JOHN MAYER
BATTLE STUDIES

This book was approved by John Mayer

Photography by Albert Watson

Arranged by Jeff Jacobson

Cherry Lane Music Company
Director of Publications/Project Editor: Mark Phillips
Project Coordinator: Rebecca Skidmore

ISBN 978-1-60378-232-6

Copyright © 2010 Cherry Lane Music Company
International Copyright Secured   All Rights Reserved

The music, text, design and graphics in this publication are protected by copyright law. Any duplication or transmission,
by any means, electronic, mechanical, photocopying, recording or otherwise, is an infringement of copyright.

Visit our website at www.cherrylaneprint.com

JOHN MAYER BATTLE STUDIES

Immediately following the release of John Mayer's *Battle Studies*, the buzz began that the seven-time Grammy-winning artist had another bulletproof hit on his hands. "*Billboard* Top 200 Chart" confirmed that *Battle Studies*, Mayer's fourth studio album, reached the highest chart position in the U.S. after a release week that catered to fans and focused on performance. *Billboard* magazine called *Battle Studies* "the best and most adventurous of his four studio albums."

Battle Studies incorporates the warmth, melodies, and simplicity of '70s and '80s California rock and pop. The album is a confessional, relaxed, and liberated album recorded in a private home in California, where Mayer lived and worked over the course of six months before wrapping at the famed Capitol Studios in Los Angeles. The album was co-produced by Mayer and Steve Jordan and released in November 2009 by Columbia Records.

Since his acclaimed debut in 2001, with *Room for Squares*, each release has earned Mayer additional accolades. Through 2003's *Heavier Things*, his work with John Mayer Trio in 2005, 2006's *Continuum*, and now, *Battle Studies*, Mayer has established himself as a musician and collaborator who exceeds genre boundaries. The guitarist, vocalist, and songwriter has earned seven Grammy Awards and sold over 12 million albums worldwide.

In May 2007 *Time* magazine placed Mayer on their "*Time* 100" list of the most influential contemporary thinkers, leaders, artists, and entertainers. For two consecutive years, *Rolling Stone* magazine featured Mayer on the cover of their annual "Guitar" issue—first with the May 2008 "Living Guitar Legends" issue and then as part of February 2007's "Guitar Heroes" roundup, showcasing Mayer with peers and icons alike.

Pairings with a range of artists is a defining trait of the musician whose collaborative streak is well known. From rock to blues, hip-hop to jazz to country, Mayer has performed and/or recorded with Eric Clapton, B.B. King, Buddy Guy, T-Bone Burnett, Herbie Hancock, the Dixie Chicks, Jay Z, Alicia Keys, and Taylor Swift. In 2005 Mayer famously toured and recorded with power players Pino Palladino and Steve Jordan as John Mayer Trio, whose live album, Try!, featured searing blues and rock.

As on *Continuum*, Mayer again took the helm as the co-producer of *Battle Studies* and crafted what is arguably one of the best rock albums of this century. The consistency with which Mayer combines word craft and melody has earned him rarefied status in popular culture as a genuine and respected songwriter and musician.

CONTENTS

HEARTBREAK WARFARE

Words and Music by
John Mayer

Copyright © 2009 Sony/ATV Music Publishing LLC and Specific Harm Music
All Rights Administered by Sony/ATV Music Publishing LLC, 8 Music Square West, Nashville, TN 37203
International Copyright Secured   All Rights Reserved

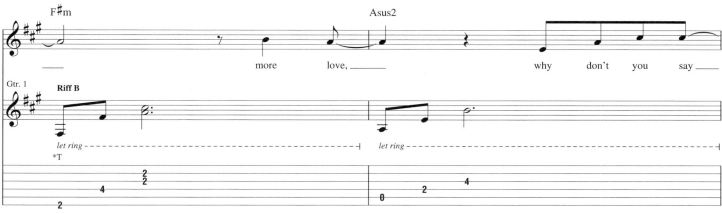

*T = Thumb on 6th string

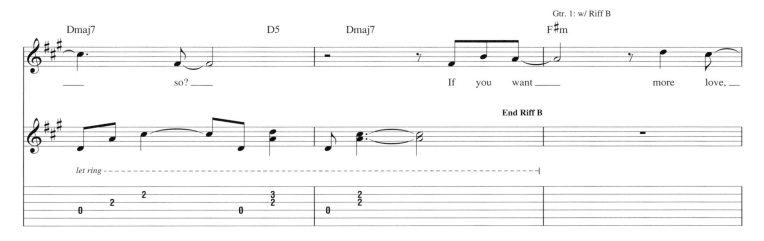

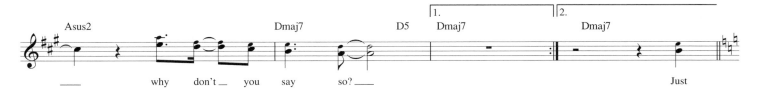

Guitar Solo

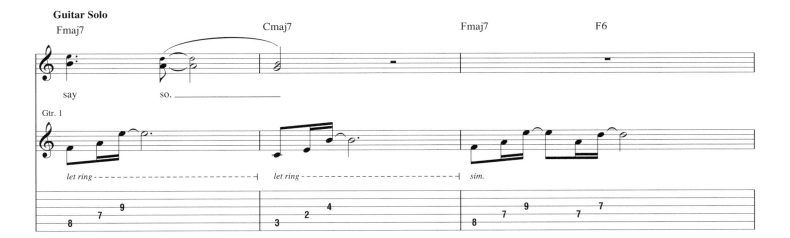

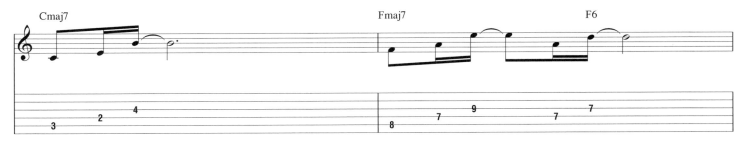

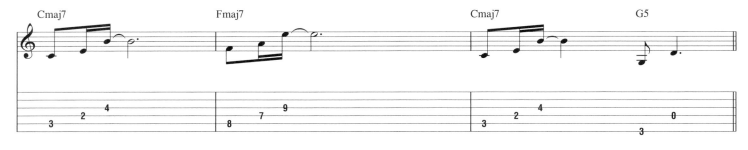

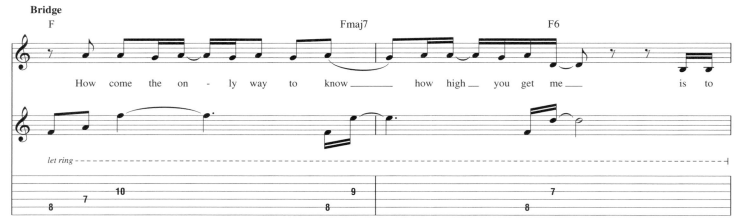

Bridge

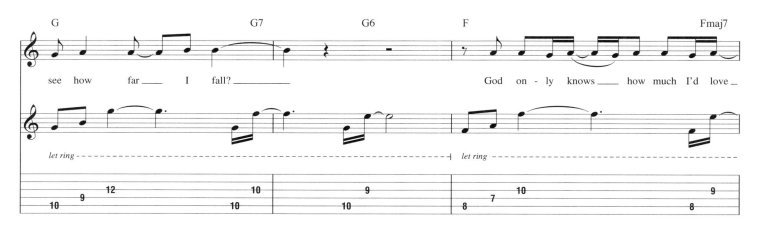

How come the on - ly way to know _____ how high ___ you get me ___ is to

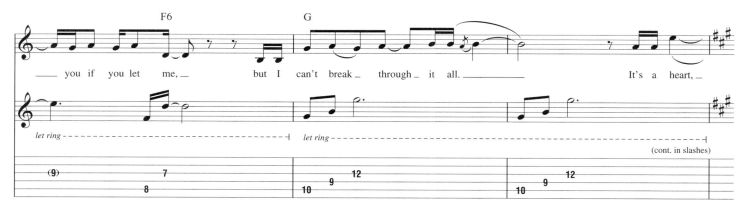

see how far ___ I fall? _____ God on - ly knows ___ how much I'd love ___

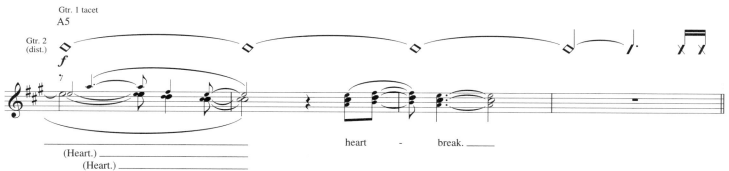

___ you if you let me, ___ but I can't break ___ through ___ it all. _____ It's a heart, ___

heart - break.

(Heart.) _____
(Heart.) _____

ALL WE EVER DO IS SAY GOODBYE

Words and Music by
John Mayer

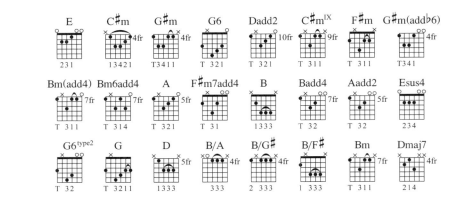

Tune down 1/2 step:
(low to high) Eb-Ab-Db-Gb-Bb-Eb

Verse

Moderately slow ♩ = 64

*Gtr. 1
(acous.)

mf

1. Just when I had you off ____ my head, ____ your
2. I bought a tick-et on ____ a plane, ____ and

*Strum primarily w/ downstrokes throughout.

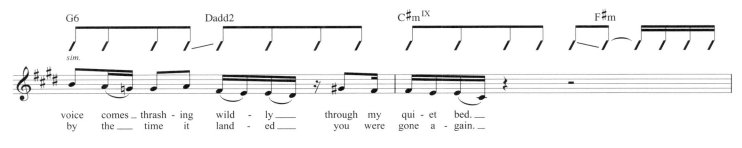

voice comes thrash-ing wild-ly ____ through my qui-et bed. ____
by the ____ time it land-ed ____ you were gone a-gain. ____

Rhy. Fig. 1

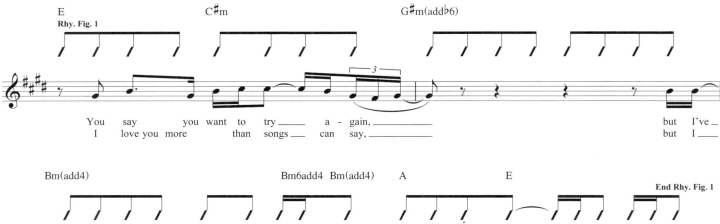

You say you want to try ____ a-gain, ____ but I've
I love you more than songs ____ can say, ____ but I ____

End Rhy. Fig. 1

____ tried ____ ev-'ry-thing ____ but ____ giv-ing in.
can't keep a-run-ning af-ter ____ yes-ter-day. ____ So...

Copyright © 2009 Sony/ATV Music Publishing LLC and Specific Harm Music
All Rights Administered by Sony/ATV Music Publishing LLC, 8 Music Square West, Nashville, TN 37203
International Copyright Secured   All Rights Reserved

HALF OF MY HEART

Words and Music by
John Mayer

Copyright © 2009 Sony/ATV Music Publishing LLC and Specific Harm Music
All Rights Administered by Sony/ATV Music Publishing LLC, 8 Music Square West, Nashville, TN 37203
International Copyright Secured   All Rights Reserved

Chorus

14

WHO SAYS

Words and Music by
John Mayer

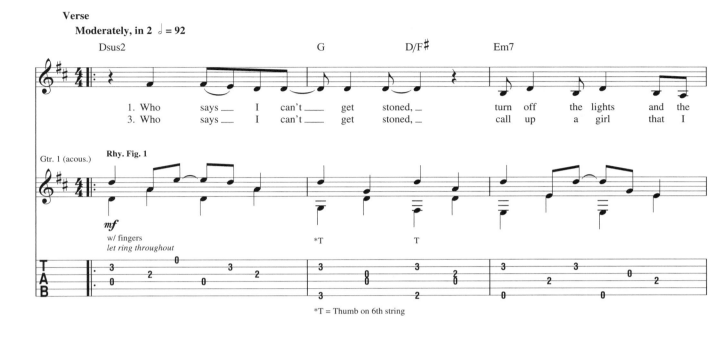

Copyright © 2009 Sony/ATV Music Publishing LLC and Specific Harm Music
All Rights Administered by Sony/ATV Music Publishing LLC, 8 Music Square West, Nashville, TN 37203
International Copyright Secured   All Rights Reserved

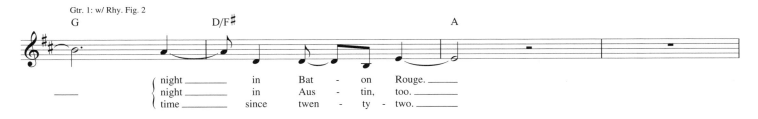

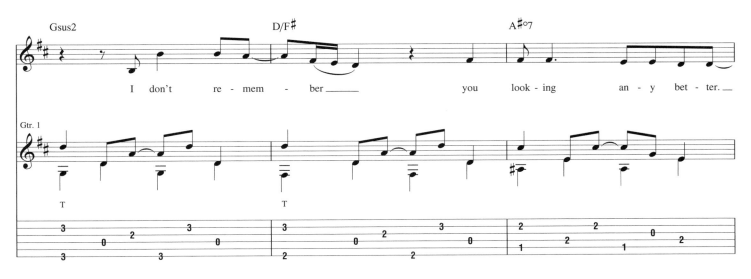

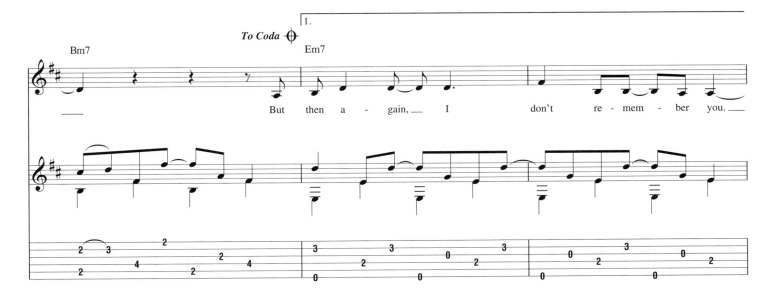

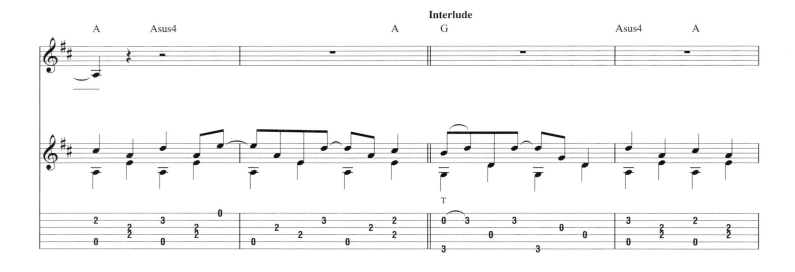

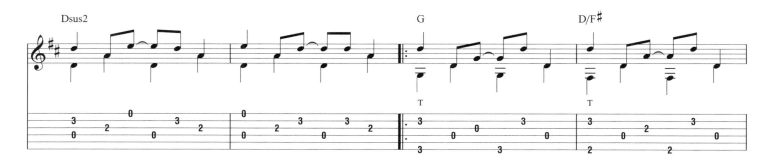

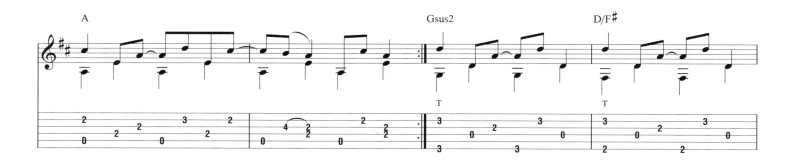

Coda

then a - gain, __ I don't re - mem - ber, don't re - mem - ber you. ___

Outro

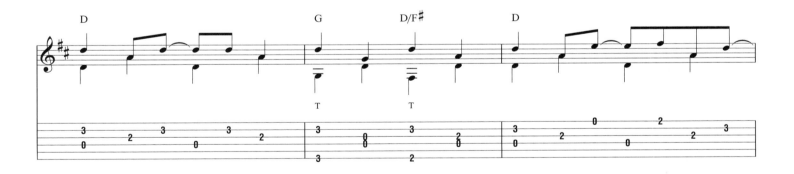

strum w/ thumb

PERFECTLY LONELY

Words and Music by
John Mayer

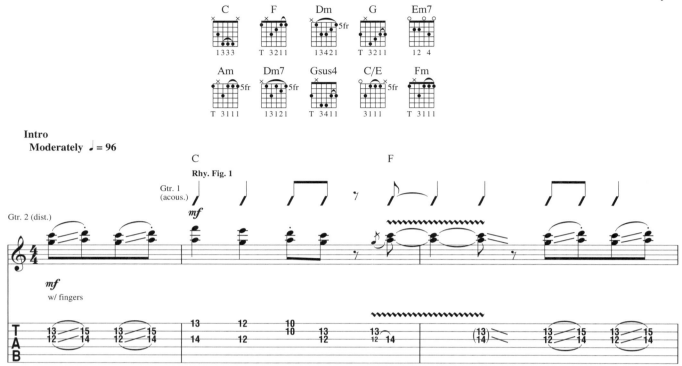

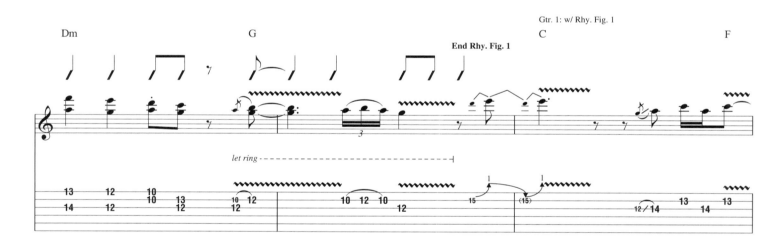

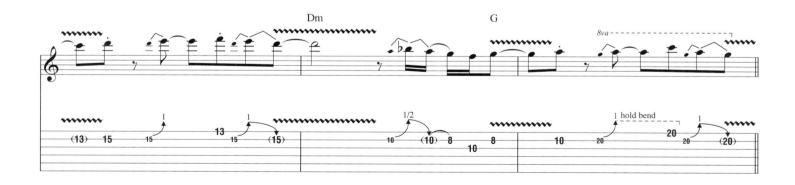

Copyright © 2009 Sony/ATV Music Publishing LLC and Specific Harm Music
All Rights Administered by Sony/ATV Music Publishing LLC, 8 Music Square West, Nashville, TN 37203
International Copyright Secured   All Rights Reserved

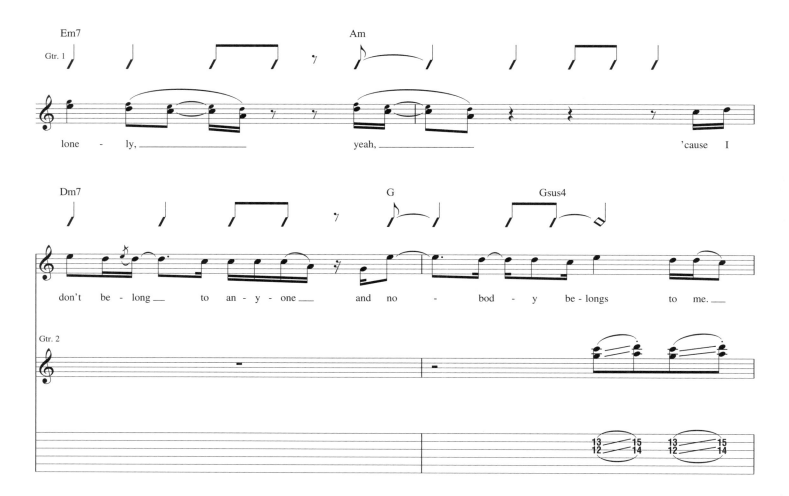

lone - ly, _____ yeah, _____ 'cause I

don't be - long __ to an - y - one __ and no - bod - y be - longs to me. __

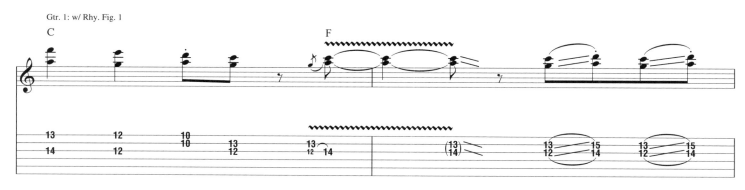

Gtr. 1: w/ Rhy. Fig. 1

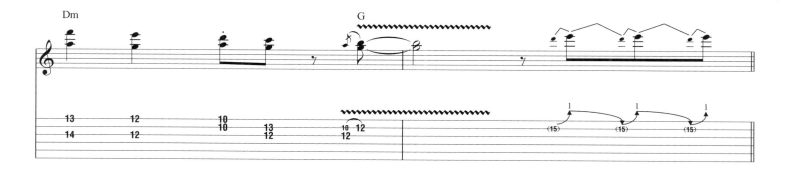

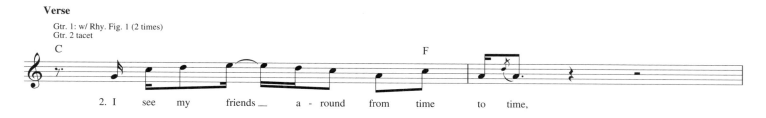

Verse

Gtr. 1: w/ Rhy. Fig. 1 (2 times)
Gtr. 2 tacet

2. I see my friends __ a - round from time to time,

24

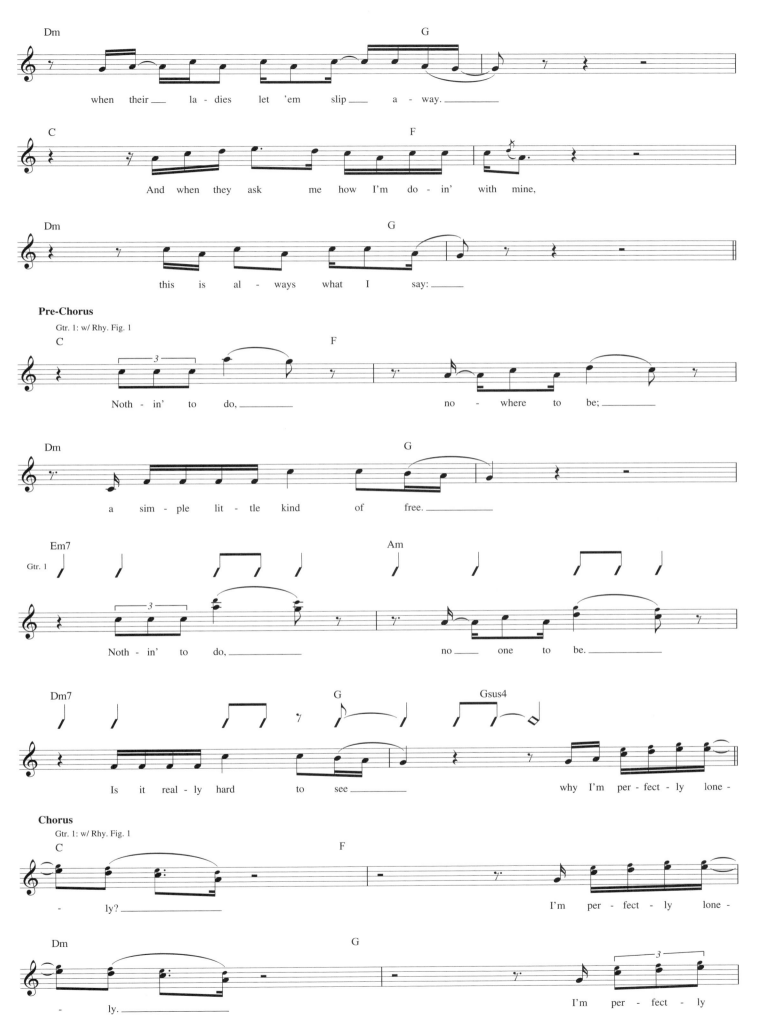

when their ___ la - dies let 'em slip ___ a - way. _____

And when they ask me how I'm do - in' with mine,

this is al - ways what I say: _____

Pre-Chorus

Gtr. 1: w/ Rhy. Fig. 1

Noth - in' to do, _____ no - where to be; _____

a sim - ple lit - tle kind of free. _____

Gtr. 1

Noth - in' to do, _____ no ___ one to be. _____

Is it real - ly hard to see _____ why I'm per - fect - ly lone -

Chorus

Gtr. 1: w/ Rhy. Fig. 1

- ly? _____ I'm per - fect - ly lone -

- ly. _____ I'm per - fect - ly

25

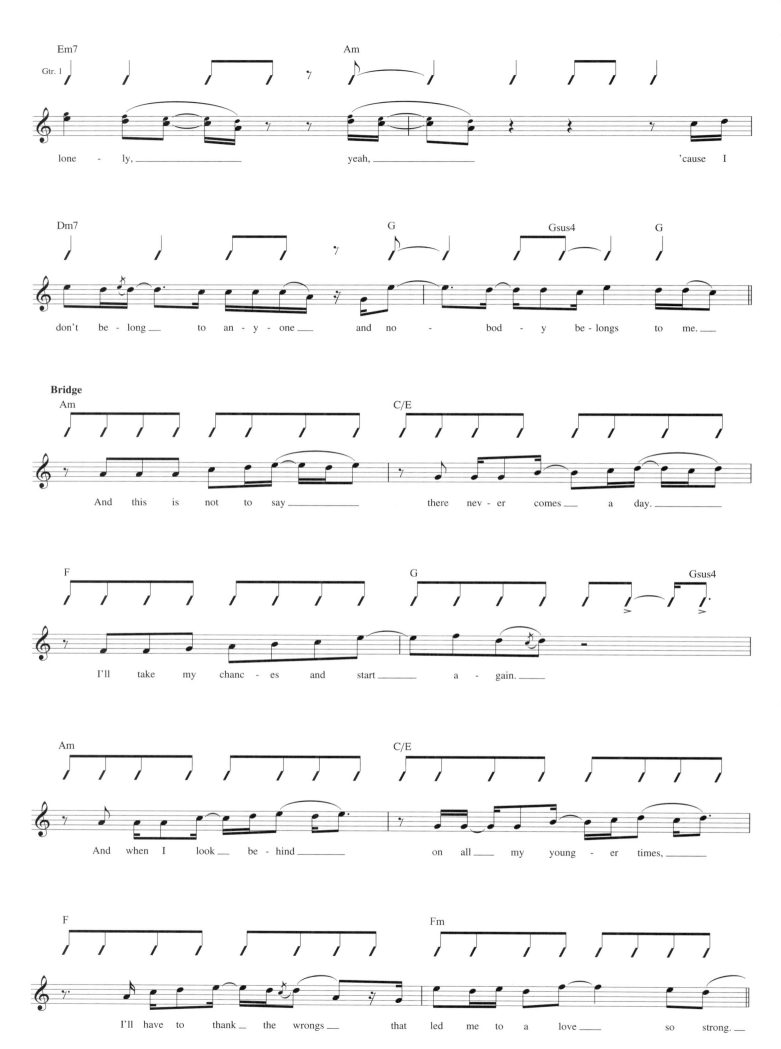

Em7   Am

Gtr. 1

lone - ly, _____ yeah, _____   'cause I

Dm7   G   Gsus4 G

don't be - long ___ to an - y - one ___ and no - bod - y be - longs to me. ___

Bridge

Am   C/E

And this is not to say _____ there nev - er comes ___ a day. _____

F   G   Gsus4

I'll take my chanc - es and start _____ a - gain. _____

Am   C/E

And when I look ___ be - hind _____ on all ___ my young - er times, _____

F   Fm

I'll have to thank ___ the wrongs ___ that led me to a love ___ so strong. ___

Outro

Gtr. 1: w/ Rhy. Fig. 1

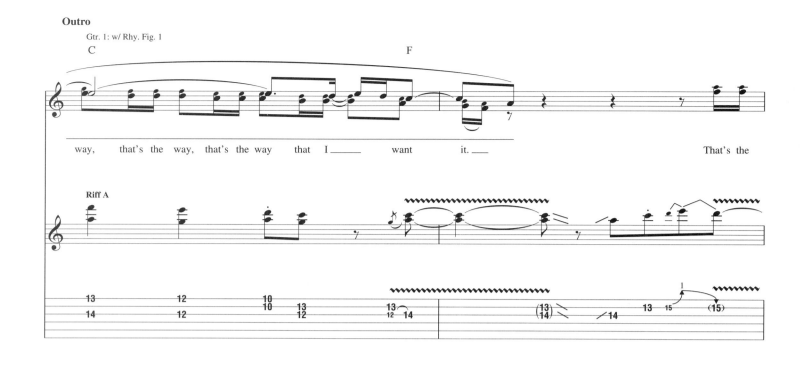

way, that's the way, that's the way that I _____ want it. _____ That's the

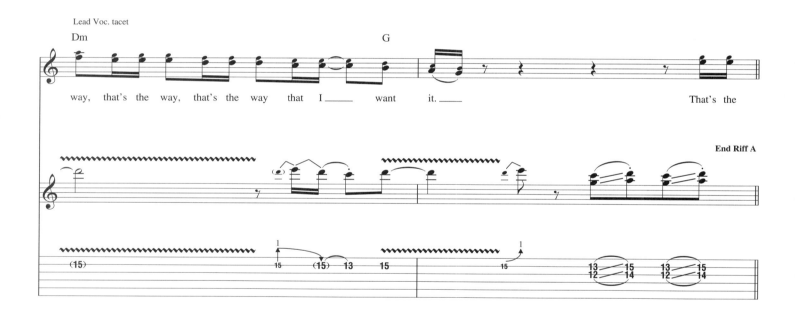

Lead Voc. tacet

way, that's the way, that's the way that I _____ want it. _____ That's the

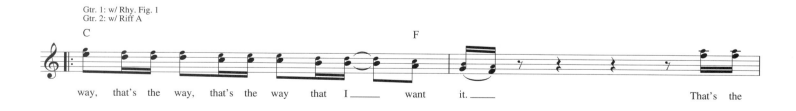

Gtr. 1: w/ Rhy. Fig. 1
Gtr. 2: w/ Riff A

way, that's the way, that's the way that I _____ want it. _____ That's the

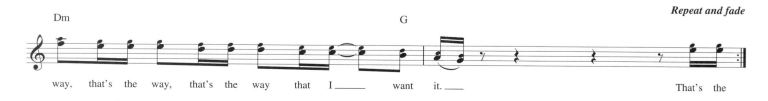

Repeat and fade

way, that's the way, that's the way that I _____ want it. _____ That's the

ASSASSIN

Words and Music by
John Mayer

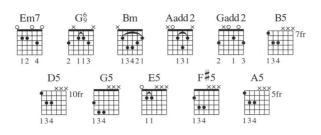

Copyright © 2009 Sony/ATV Music Publishing LLC and Specific Harm Music
All Rights Administered by Sony/ATV Music Publishing LLC, 8 Music Square West, Nashville, TN 37203
International Copyright Secured   All Rights Reserved

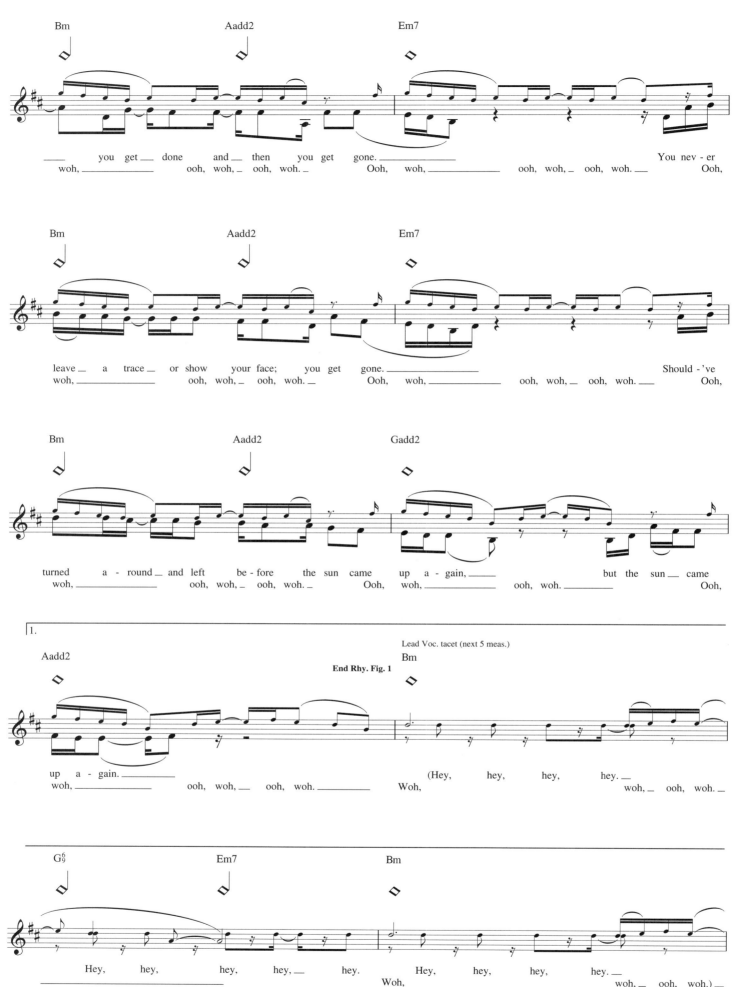

Hey, hey, hey, hey.) ___

2. In - to the morn up a - gain. ___
woh, ___ ooh, woh, ___ ooh, woh.)

Chorus

I was ___ a kill - er, was ___ the best ___ they'd ev - er ___ seen. ___

I'd steal ___ your heart ___ be - fore ___ you ev - er heard ___ a ___ thing. ___

I'm an ___ as - sas - sin and ___ I had ___ a job ___ to ___ do. ___

To Coda

Lit - tle did I know ___ that girl ___ was an ___ as - sas - sin ___ too. ___

CROSSROADS

Words and Music by
Robert Johnson

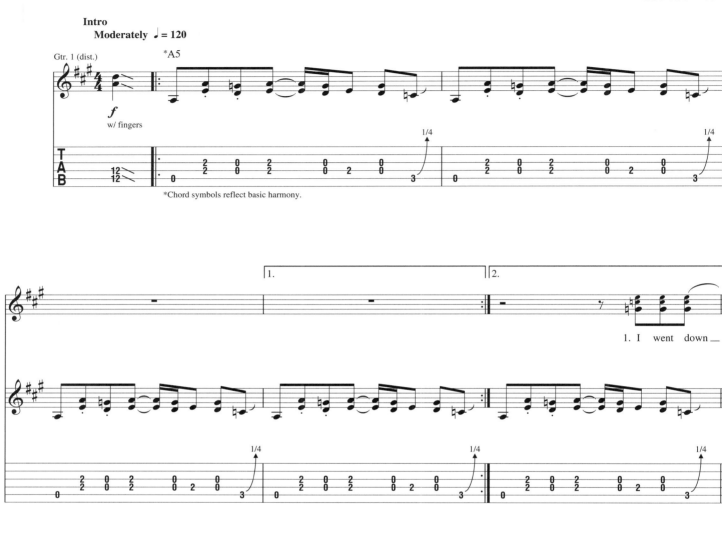

*Chord symbols reflect basic harmony.

Copyright © (1978), 1990, 1991 MPCA King Of Spades (SESAC) and Claud L. Johnson (SESAC)
Administered by MPCA Music, LLC
All Rights Reserved

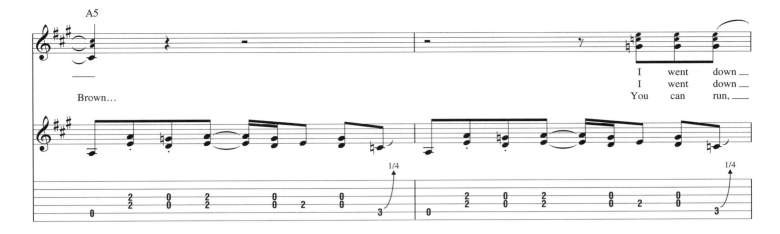

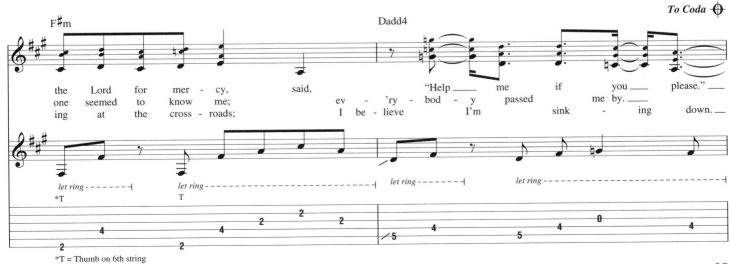

*T = Thumb on 6th string

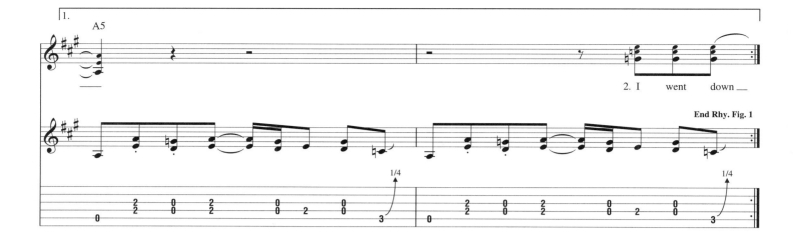

2. I went down ___

2. A5 ... N.C.

Guitar Solo
Gtr. 1: w/ Rhy. Fig. 1 (2 times)

1. 2. *D.S. al Coda*

3. You can run, ___

WAR OF MY LIFE

Words and Music by
John Mayer

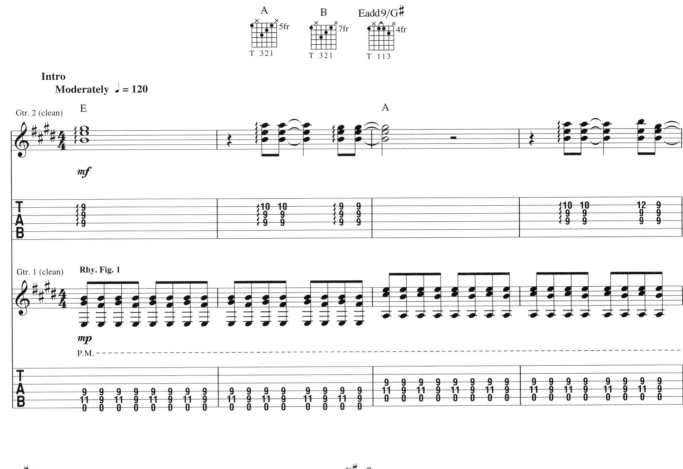

*T = Thumb on 6th string

Copyright © 2009 Sony/ATV Music Publishing LLC and Specific Harm Music
All Rights Administered by Sony/ATV Music Publishing LLC, 8 Music Square West, Nashville, TN 37203
International Copyright Secured   All Rights Reserved

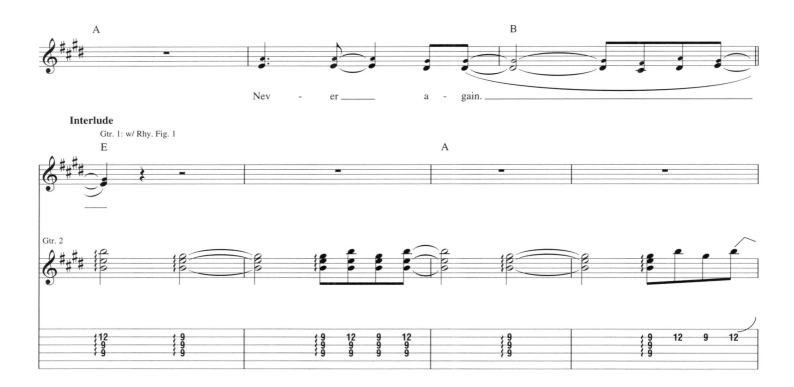

Nev - er _____ a - gain. _____

Interlude

Gtr. 1: w/ Rhy. Fig. 1

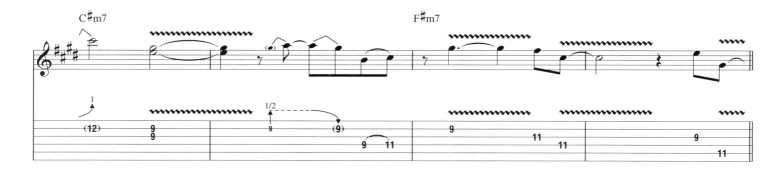

Breakdown-Chorus

Gtr. 2 tacet

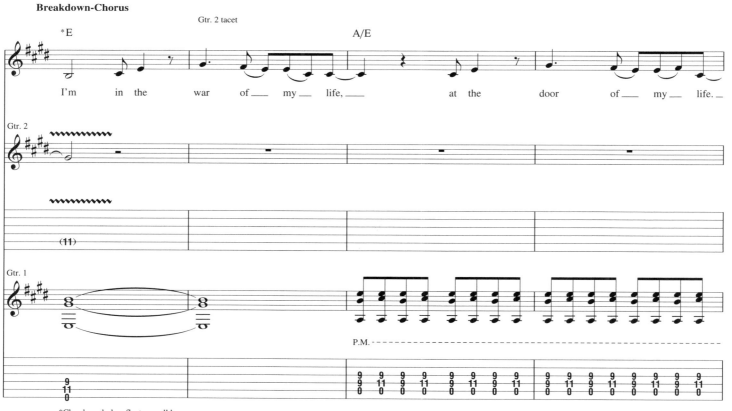

I'm in the war of __ my __ life, _____ at the door of __ my __ life.

*Chord symbols reflect overall harmony.

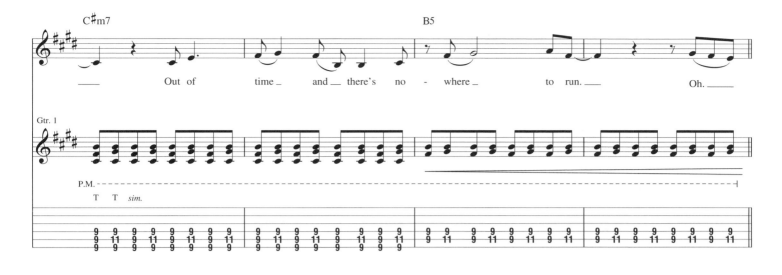

Out of time __ and __ there's no - where __ to run. __ Oh. __

P.M. -

T T *sim.*

Chorus

Gtr. 1: w/ Rhy. Fig. 1

I'm in the war __ of __ my __ life; __ I'm at the core __

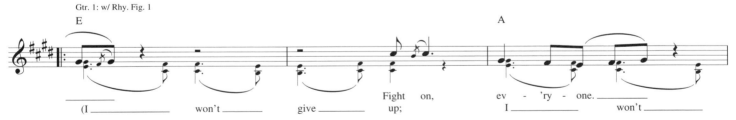

__ of __ my life. Got no __ choice __ but __ to fight

till __ it's done. __ So fight on. __

Outro

Gtr. 1: w/ Rhy. Fig. 1

(I __ won't __ give __ up; Fight on, ev - 'ry - one. I __ won't __

Fight on. __ Got no __ choice __ but __ to fight
run. I __ won't __ stop __ for

Repeat and fade

till __ it's done. __ Fight on. __
an - till __ it's y __ - one.)

41

EDGE OF DESIRE

Words and Music by
John Mayer

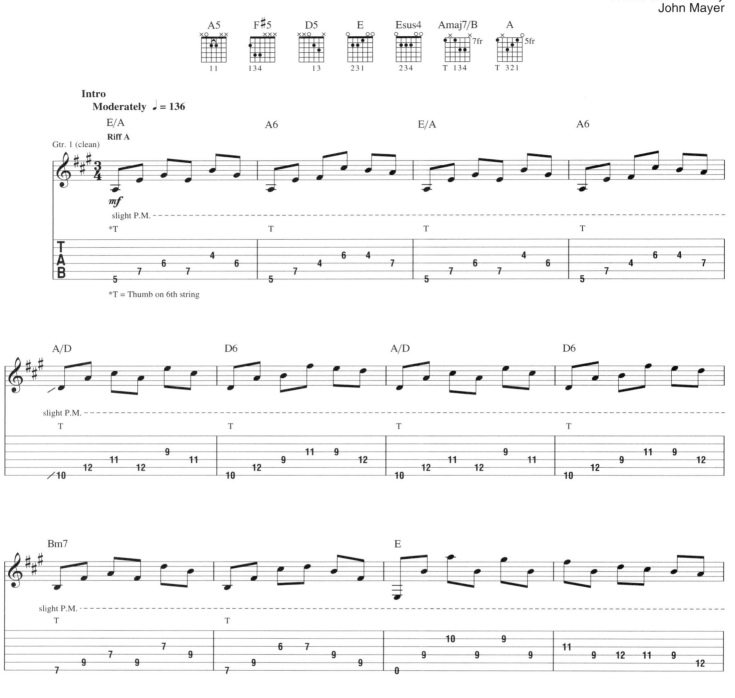

Copyright © 2009 Sony/ATV Music Publishing LLC and Specific Harm Music
All Rights Administered by Sony/ATV Music Publishing LLC, 8 Music Square West, Nashville, TN 37203
International Copyright Secured   All Rights Reserved

Chorus

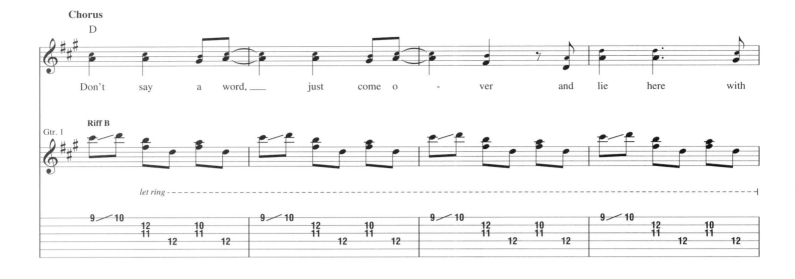

Don't say a word, ___ just come o - ver and lie here with

me. ___ 'Cause

Gtr. 1: w/ Riff B (2 1/2 times)

I'm just a - bout ___ to set ___ fi - re to ev - 'ry - thing I

see. ___ I want you so ___ bad, ___

___ I'll go ___ back ___ on the things ___ I be - lieve. ___

There, I just ___ said ___ it. I'm scared you'll for - get ___ a - bout

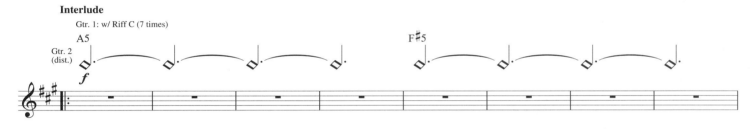

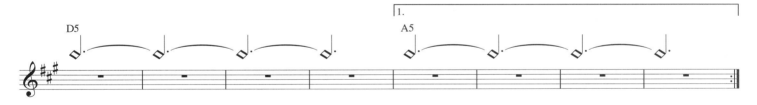

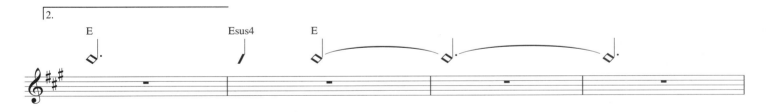

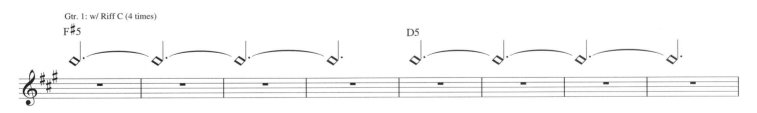

Chorus

Gtr. 1: w/ Riff B (1st 4 meas.)

D5

Don't say a word; _____ just come o - ver and lie here with

Gtr. 1: w/ Riff C

A5

me. _____ 'Cause

Gtr. 1: w/ Riff B (1st 4 meas.)

D5

I'm just a - bout _____ to set _____ fi - re to ev - 'ry - thing I

Gtr. 1: w/ Riff C

A5

Gtr. 1: w/ Riff B (1st 4 meas.)

D5

see. _____ I want _____ you so _____ bad _____

Gtr. 1: w/ Riff C

A5

_____ I'll go _____ back _____ on the things _____ I be - lieve. _____

Gtr. 1: w/ Riff B (1st 4 meas.)

D5

Amaj7/B

There, I just _____ said _____ it; _____ I'm scared you'll for - get _____

Gtr. 1: w/ Riff C

A5

_____ a - bout _____ me. _____

Outro

Gtr. 1: w/ Riff C (2 times)
Gtr. 2 tacet

A

A

Gtr. 1

8

46

DO YOU KNOW ME

Words and Music by
John Mayer

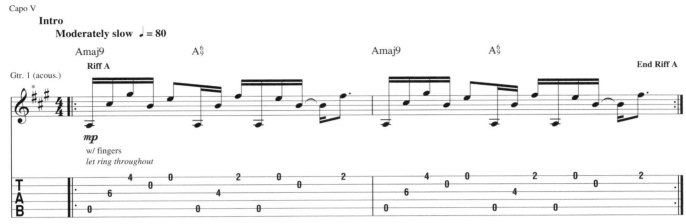

Capo V

Intro

Moderately slow ♩ = 80

*All music sounds a perfect 4th higher than indicated due to capo. Capoed fret is "0" in tab.

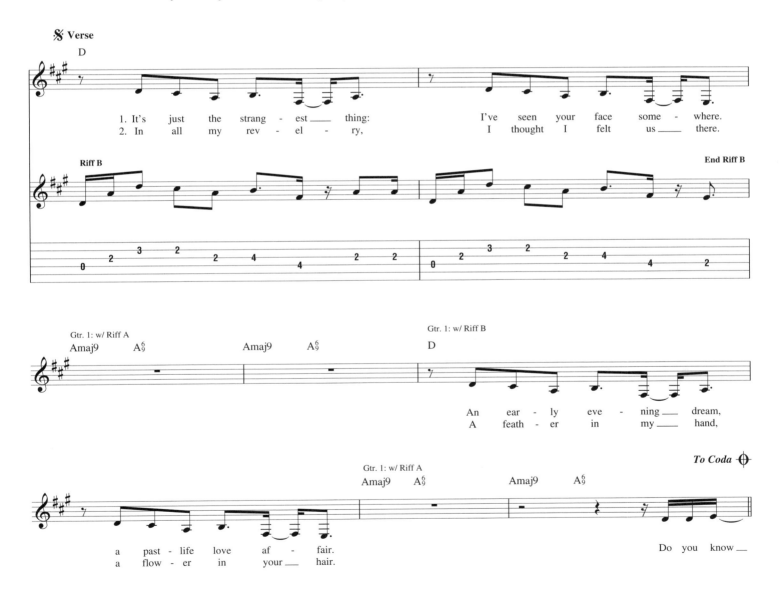

1. It's just the strang - est ___ thing: I've seen your face some - where.
2. In all my rev - el - ry, I thought I felt us ___ there.

An ear - ly eve - ning ___ dream,
A feath - er in my ___ hand,

a past - life love af - fair.
a flow - er in your ___ hair.

Do you know ___

Copyright © 2009 Sony/ATV Music Publishing LLC and Specific Harm Music
All Rights Administered by Sony/ATV Music Publishing LLC, 8 Music Square West, Nashville, TN 37203
International Copyright Secured   All Rights Reserved

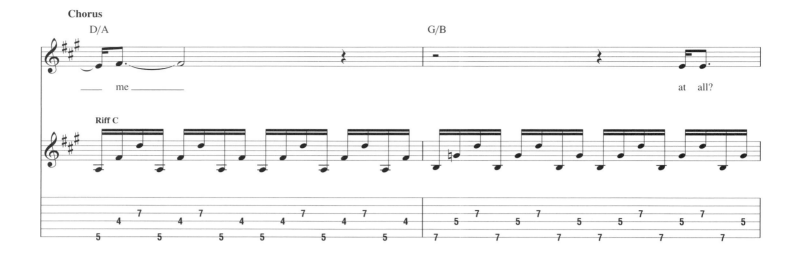

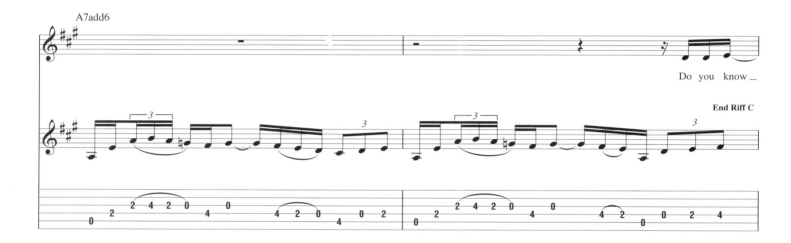

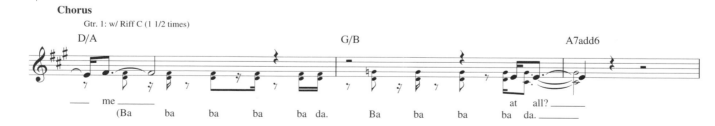

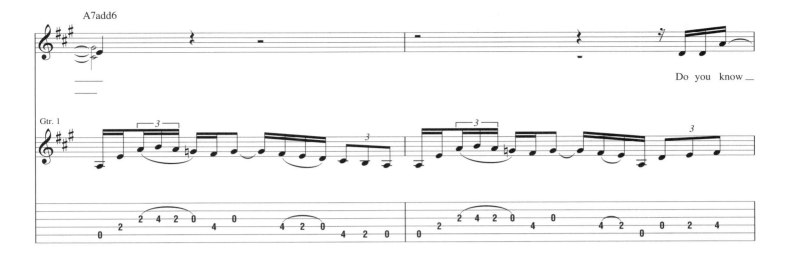

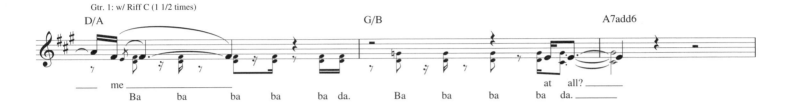

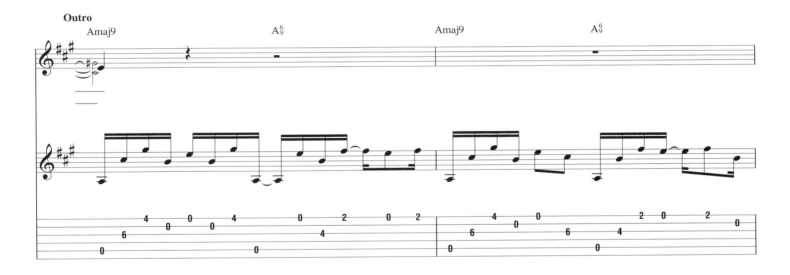

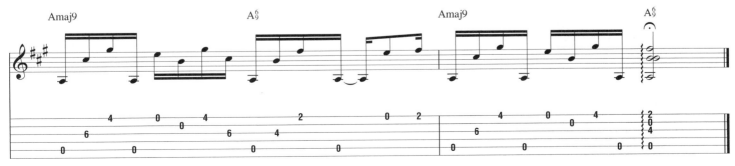

FRIENDS, LOVERS OR NOTHING

Words and Music by
John Mayer

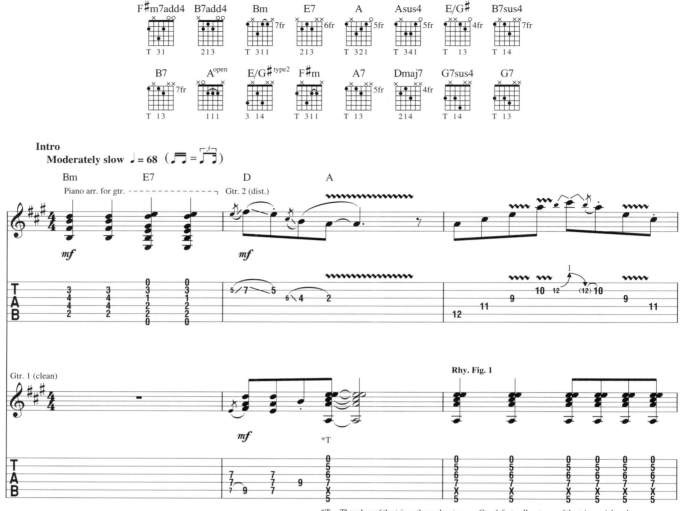

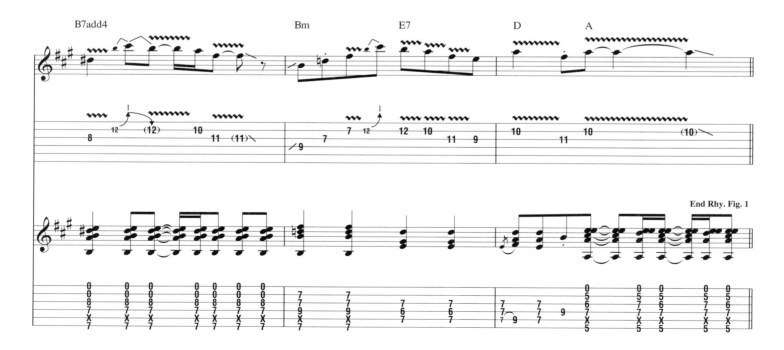

*T = Thumb on 6th string; throughout song, Gtr. 1 frets all notes on 6th string w/ thumb.

Copyright © 2009 Sony/ATV Music Publishing LLC and Specific Harm Music
All Rights Administered by Sony/ATV Music Publishing LLC, 8 Music Square West, Nashville, TN 37203
International Copyright Secured   All Rights Reserved

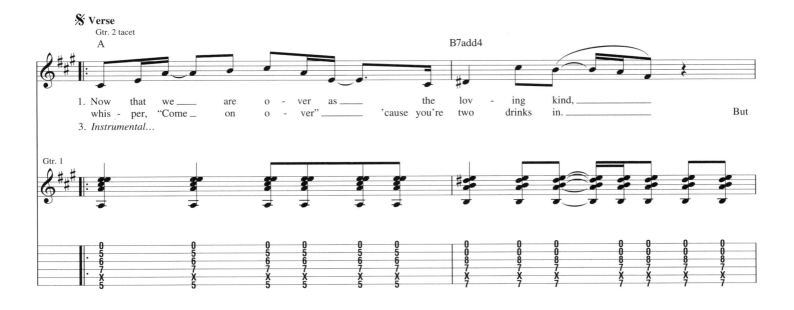

1. Now that we ___ are o - ver as ___ the lov - ing kind, ___
whis - per, "Come ___ on o - ver" ___ 'cause you're two drinks in. ___ But
3. *Instrumental…*

we'll be dream - ing ways ___ to keep ___ the good a - live. ___
in the morn - ing I ___ will say ___ good - bye a - gain.

On - ly when ___ we want ___ is not ___ to com - pro - mise, ___
Think we'll nev - er fall ___ in - to ___ a jeal - ous game? ___ The

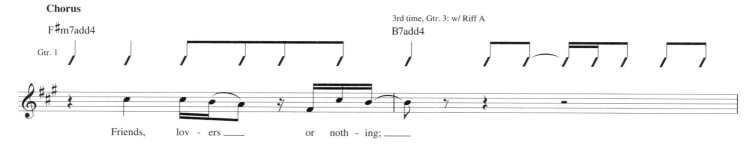

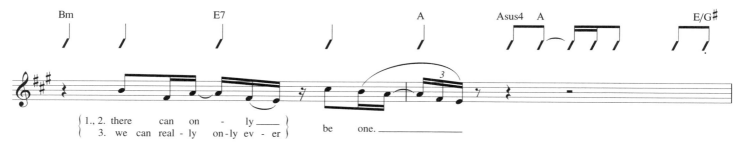

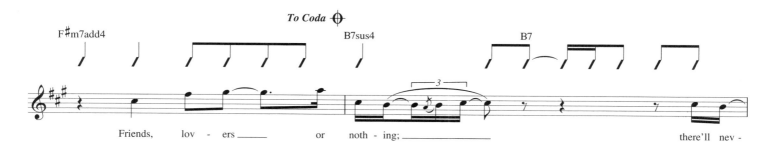

er be ___ an in - be - tween, ___ so give it up. ___

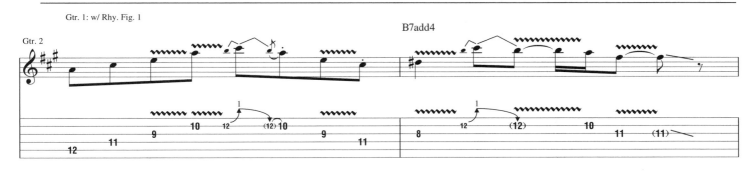

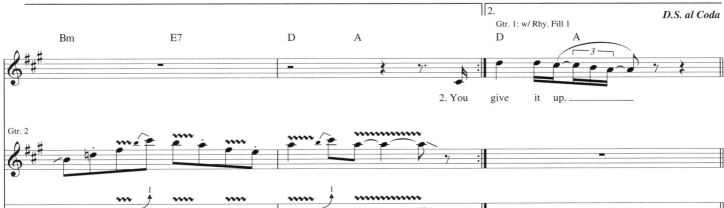

2. You give it up. ___

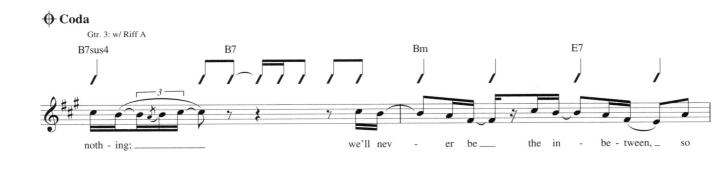

noth - ing; ___ we'll nev - er be ___ the in - be - tween, ___ so

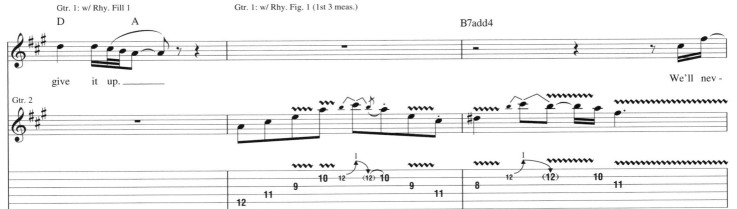

give it up. ___

We'll nev -

Guitar Notation Legend

Guitar music can be notated three different ways: on a *musical staff*, in *tablature*, and in *rhythm slashes*.

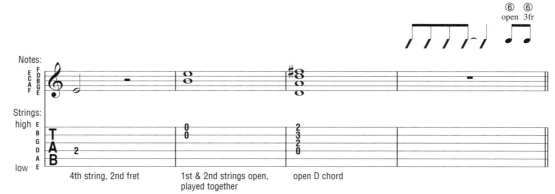

RHYTHM SLASHES are written above the staff. Strum chords in the rhythm indicated. Use the chord diagrams found at the top of the first page of the transcription for the appropriate chord voicings. Round noteheads indicate single notes.

THE MUSICAL STAFF shows pitches and rhythms and is divided by bar lines into measures. Pitches are named after the first seven letters of the alphabet.

TABLATURE graphically represents the guitar fingerboard. Each horizontal line represents a string, and each number represents a fret.

4th string, 2nd fret   1st & 2nd strings open, played together   open D chord

HALF-STEP BEND: Strike the note and bend up 1/2 step.

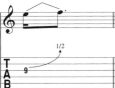

WHOLE-STEP BEND: Strike the note and bend up one step.

GRACE NOTE BEND: Strike the note and immediately bend up as indicated.

SLIGHT (MICROTONE) BEND: Strike the note and bend up 1/4 step.

BEND AND RELEASE: Strike the note and bend up as indicated, then release back to the original note. Only the first note is struck.

PRE-BEND: Bend the note as indicated, then strike it.

VIBRATO: The string is vibrated by rapidly bending and releasing the note with the fretting hand.

WIDE VIBRATO: The pitch is varied to a greater degree by vibrating with the fretting hand.

HAMMER-ON: Strike the first (lower) note with one finger, then sound the higher note (on the same string) with another finger by fretting it without picking.

PULL-OFF: Place both fingers on the notes to be sounded. Strike the first note and without picking, pull the finger off to sound the second (lower) note.

LEGATO SLIDE: Strike the first note and then slide the same fret-hand finger up or down to the second note. The second note is not struck.

SHIFT SLIDE: Same as legato slide, except the second note is struck.

TRILL: Very rapidly alternate between the notes indicated by continuously hammering on and pulling off.

TAPPING: Hammer ("tap") the fret indicated with the pick-hand index or middle finger and pull off to the note fretted by the fret hand.

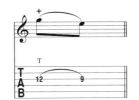

NATURAL HARMONIC: Strike the note while the fret-hand lightly touches the string directly over the fret indicated.

PINCH HARMONIC: The note is fretted normally and a harmonic is produced by adding the edge of the thumb or the tip of the index finger of the pick hand to the normal pick attack.

PICK SCRAPE: The edge of the pick is rubbed down (or up) the string, producing a scratchy sound.

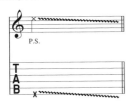

MUFFLED STRINGS: A percussive sound is produced by laying the fret hand across the string(s) without depressing, and striking them with the pick hand.

PALM MUTING: The note is partially muted by the pick hand lightly touching the string(s) just before the bridge.

RAKE: Drag the pick across the strings indicated with a single motion.

TREMOLO PICKING: The note is picked as rapidly and continuously as possible.

VIBRATO BAR DIVE AND RETURN: The pitch of the note or chord is dropped a specified number of steps (in rhythm), then returned to the original pitch.

VIBRATO BAR SCOOP: Depress the bar just before striking the note, then quickly release the bar.

VIBRATO BAR DIP: Strike the note and then immediately drop a specified number of steps, then release back to the original pitch.

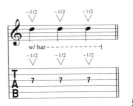

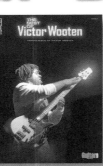

THE HOTTEST TAB SONGBOOKS AVAILABLE FOR GUITAR & BASS!

PLAY IT LIKE IT IS GUITAR WITH TABLATURE — NOTE-FOR-NOTE TRANSCRIPTIONS

PLAY IT LIKE IT IS BASS WITH TABLATURE — NOTE-FOR-NOTE TRANSCRIPTIONS

from

cherry lane music company

For complete listing of Cherry Lane titles available, including contents listings, please visit our website at
www.cherrylane.com

Guitar Transcriptions

02500702	**Best of Black Label Society**	$22.95
02500842	**Black Label Society – Mafia**	$19.95
02500116	**Black Sabbath – Riff by Riff**	$14.95
02500882	**Blues Masters by the Bar**	$19.95
02500921	**Best of Joe Bonamassa**	$22.95
02501272	**Bush – 16 Stone**	$21.95
02500179	**Mary Chapin Carpenter** Authentic Guitar Style of	$16.95
02500336	**Eric Clapton – Just the Riffs**	$12.99
02506319	**Eric Clapton – Riff by Riff**	$17.95
02500684	**Dashboard Confessional –** A Mark • A Mission • A Brand • A Scar	$19.95
02500689	**Dashboard Confessional –** The Places You Have Come to Fear the Most	$17.95
02500843	**Dashboard Confessional –** The Swiss Army Romance	$17.95
02506878	**John Denver Anthology** for Easy Guitar Revised Edition	$15.95
02506901	**John Denver Authentic Guitar Style**	$14.95
02500984	**John Denver – Folk Singer**	$19.95
02506928	**John Denver –** Greatest Hits for Fingerstyle Guitar	$14.95
02500632	**John Denver Collection Strum & Sing Series**	$9.95
02500652	**Dio – 5 of the Best**	$9.95
02500607	**The Best of Dispatch**	$19.95
02501147	**50 Easy Spanish Guitar Solos**	$14.95
02500198	**Best of Foreigner**	$19.95
02500990	**Donavon Frankenreiter**	$19.95
02501242	**Guns N' Roses – Anthology**	$24.95
02506953	**Guns N' Roses – Appetite for Destruction**	$22.95
02501286	**Guns N' Roses Complete, Volume 1**	$24.95
02501287	**Guns N' Roses Complete, Volume 2**	$24.95
02506211	**Guns N' Roses – 5 of the Best, Vol. 1**	$12.95
02506975	**Guns N' Roses – GN'R Lies**	$19.95
02500299	**Guns N' Roses – Live Era '87-'93 Highlights**	$24.95
02501193	**Guns N' Roses – Use Your Illusion I**	$24.95
02501194	**Guns N' Roses – Use Your Illusion II**	$24.95
02506325	**Metallica – The Art of Kirk Hammett**	$17.95
02500939	**Hawthorne Heights –** The Silence in Black and White	$19.95
02500458	**Best of Warren Haynes**	$22.95
02500476	**Warren Haynes – Guide to Slide Guitar**	$17.95
02500387	**Best of Heart**	$19.95
02500016	**The Art of James Hetfield**	$17.95
02500007	**Hole – Celebrity Skin**	$19.95
02500873	**Jazz for the Blues Guitarist**	$14.95
02500554	**Jack Johnson – Brushfire Fairytales**	$19.95
02500831	**Jack Johnson – In Between Dreams**	$19.95
02500653	**Jack Johnson – On and On**	$19.95

02500858	**Jack Johnson – Strum & Sing**	$10.95
02500380	**Lenny Kravitz – Greatest Hits**	$19.95
02500024	**Best of Lenny Kravitz**	$19.95
02500129	**Adrian Legg – Pickin' 'n' Squintin'**	$19.95
02500362	**Best of Little Feat**	$19.95
02501094	**Hooks That Kill –** The Best of Mick Mars & Mötley Crüe	$19.95
02500305	**Best of The Marshall Tucker Band**	$19.95
02501077	**Dave Matthews Band – Anthology**	$24.95
02501357	**Dave Matthews Band –** Before These Crowded Streets	$19.95
02500553	**Dave Matthews Band – Busted Stuff**	$22.95
02501279	**Dave Matthews Band – Crash**	$19.95
02500389	**Dave Matthews Band – Everyday**	$19.95
02501266	**Dave Matthews Band –** Under the Table and Dreaming	$19.95
02500131	**Dave Matthews/Tim Reynolds –** Live at Luther College, Vol. 1	$19.95
02500611	**Dave Matthews/Tim Reynolds –** Live at Luther College, Vol. 2	$22.95
02500986	**John Mayer – Continuum**	$22.95
02500705	**John Mayer – Heavier Things**	$22.95
02500529	**John Mayer – Room for Squares**	$22.95
02506965	**Metallica – ...And Justice for All**	$22.95
02501267	**Metallica – Death Magnetic**	$24.95
02506210	**Metallica – 5 of the Best/Vol.1**	$12.95
02506235	**Metallica – 5 of the Best/Vol. 2**	$12.95
02500070	**Metallica – Garage, Inc.**	$24.95
02507018	**Metallica – Kill 'Em All**	$19.95
02501232	**Metallica – Live: Binge & Purge**	$19.95
02501275	**Metallica – Load**	$24.95
02507920	**Metallica – Master of Puppets**	$19.95
02501195	**Metallica – Metallica**	$22.95
02501297	**Metallica – ReLoad**	$24.95
02507019	**Metallica – Ride the Lightning**	$19.95
02500279	**Metallica – S&M Highlights**	$24.95
02500638	**Metallica – St. Anger**	$24.95
02500577	**Molly Hatchet – 5 of the Best**	$9.95
02500846	**Best of Steve Morse Band and Dixie Dregs**	$19.95
02500765	**Jason Mraz – Waiting for My Rocket to Come**	$19.95
02500448	**Best of Ted Nugent**	$19.95
02500707	**Ted Nugent – Legendary Licks**	$19.95
02500844	**Best of O.A.R. (Of a Revolution)**	$22.95
02500348	**Ozzy Osbourne – Blizzard of Ozz**	$19.95
02501277	**Ozzy Osbourne – Diary of a Madman**	$19.95
02507904	**Ozzy Osbourne/Randy Rhoads Tribute**	$22.95
02500524	**The Bands of Ozzfest**	$16.95
02500525	**More Bands of Ozzfest**	$16.95
02500680	**Don't Stop Believin':** The Steve Perry Anthology	$22.95

02500025	**Primus Anthology – A-N (Guitar/Bass)**	$19.95
02500091	**Primus Anthology – O-Z (Guitar/Bass)**	$19.95
02500468	**Primus – Sailing the Seas of Cheese**	$19.95
02500875	**Queens of the Stone Age –** Lullabies to Paralyze	$24.95
02500608	**Queens of the Stone Age – Songs for the Deaf**	$19.95
02500659	**The Best of Bonnie Raitt**	$24.95
02501268	**Joe Satriani**	$22.95
02501299	**Joe Satriani – Crystal Planet**	$24.95
02500306	**Joe Satriani – Engines of Creation**	$22.95
02501205	**Joe Satriani – The Extremist**	$22.95
02507029	**Joe Satriani – Flying in a Blue Dream**	$22.95
02501155	**Joe Satriani – Professor Satchafunkilus** and the Musterion of Rock	$24.95
02500544	**Joe Satriani – Strange Beautiful Music**	$22.95
02500920	**Joe Satriani – Super Colossal**	$22.95
02506959	**Joe Satriani – Surfing with the Alien**	$19.95
02500560	**Joe Satriani Anthology**	$24.95
02501255	**Best of Joe Satriani**	$19.95
02501238	**Sepultura – Chaos A.D.**	$19.95
02500188	**Best of the Brian Setzer Orchestra**	$19.95
02500985	**Sex Pistols – Never Mind the Bollocks,** Here's the Sex Pistols	$19.95
02501230	**Soundgarden – Superunknown**	$19.95
02500799	**Tenacious D**	$19.95
02501035	**Tenacious D – The Pick of Destiny**	$19.95
02501263	**Tesla – Time's Making Changes**	$19.95
02501147	**30 Easy Spanish Guitar Solos**	$14.95
02500561	**Learn Funk Guitar with** Tower of Power's Jeff Tamelier	$19.95
02501007	**Keith Urban –** Love, Pain & The Whole Crazy Thing	$24.95
02500636	**The White Stripes – Elephant**	$19.95
02501095	**The White Stripes – Icky Thump**	$19.95
02500583	**The White Stripes – White Blood Cells**	$19.95
02501092	**Wilco – Sky Blue Sky**	$22.95
02500431	**Best of Johnny Winter**	$19.95
02500949	**Wolfmother**	$22.95
02500199	**Best of Zakk Wylde**	$22.95
02500700	**Zakk Wylde – Legendary Licks**	$19.95

Bass Transcriptions

02501108	**Bass Virtuosos**	$19.95
02500117	**Black Sabbath – Riff by Riff Bass**	$17.95
02506966	**Guns N' Roses – Appetite for Destruction**	$19.95
02500639	**Metallica – St. Anger**	$19.95
02500771	**Best of Rancid for Bass**	$17.95
02501120	**Best of Tower of Power for Bass**	$19.95
02500317	**Victor Wooten Songbook**	$22.95

Transcribed Scores

02500424	**The Best of Metallica**	$24.95
02500715	**Mr. Big – Greatest Hits**	$24.95
02500883	**Mr. Big – Lean into It**	$24.95

See your local music dealer or contact:

cherry lane music company

EXCLUSIVELY DISTRIBUTED BY
HAL•LEONARD CORPORATION
7777 W. BLUEMOUND RD. P.O. BOX 13819 MILWAUKEE, WI 53213

Prices, contents, and availability subject to change without notice.

0909